OXFORD CONNECTIONS

CHILDREN IN WORLD WAR 2

Kenna Bourke

Series editor **Sue Palmer**

D0247283

OXFORD
UNIVERSITY PRESS

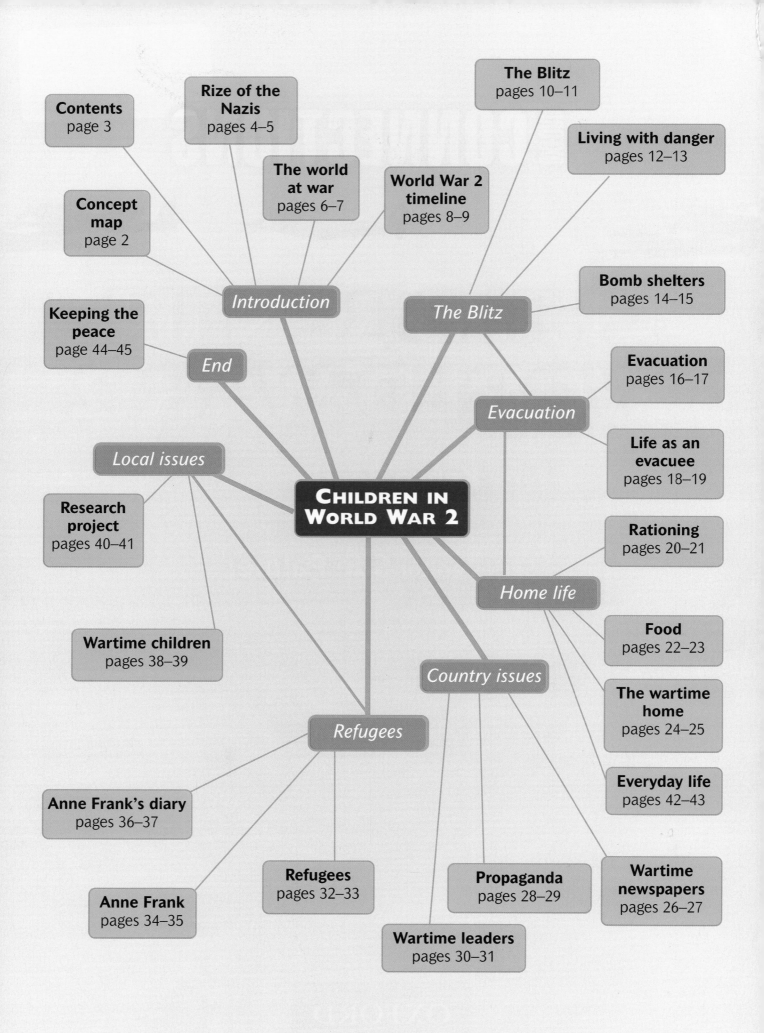

Contents

My favourite thing in the book was how you ask other people in the country about what they felt like in the war. And if children read it, they will learn a lot about the war. When I was in the house I got a lot of information about the war.

Thomas Hymers
Actor in *The 1940s House*, Channel 4

I enjoyed the entire book, especially the 'Living with danger' chapter. You found the observers' views and not just something from a reference book. 'Rationing' was a very interesting chapter, it was interesting to see what it was like in other countries too. The whole book is extremely interesting.

Ben Hymers
Actor in *The 1940s House*, Channel 4

Rise of the Nazis

In 1933, Adolf Hitler was made Chancellor of Germany. When the President of Germany died in 1934, Hitler combined the posts of Chancellor and President, and became overall leader of Germany. He and his followers, who were called the **Nazi** party, believed that the Germans were a 'master race', better than all others, and that they should rule over other people. In 1938 and 1939, Hitler's army marched into Austria and Czechoslovakia and took them over.

Ein Volk, ein Reich, ein Führer!

Hitler was widely know as the Führer (a German word for leader) of Germany.

Nazi poster for youth hostel campaign

Nazi propaganda was aimed at people of all ages.

THE DAILY MIRROR, Friday, August 3, 1934.   Broadcasting - Page 24

Daily Mirror

THE DAILY PICTURE NEWSPAPER WITH THE LARGEST NET SALE

EX - KAISER'S TRIBUTE TO HINDENBURG — Page 3

No. 9,574   Registered at the G.P.O. as a Newspaper.   FRIDAY, AUGUST 3, 1934.   One Penny

HITLER MASTER OF GERMANY
Decree an Hour After Death of Hindenburg

SOLDIERS' OATH OF "LOYALTY TO DEATH" TO NEW PRESIDENT

When Hindenburg, the President of Germany, died Hitler became leader of Germany.

For a long time, people in other European countries thought they would be able to reason with Hitler, and live in peace. Eventually, however, they realized that Hitler was not a reasonable man. It became clear that, unless he was stopped, Hitler and his Nazis would try to take over the whole of Europe.

In September 1939, Hitler invaded Poland. Britain and France, together with Australia and New Zealand, declared war on Germany.

Hitler's invasion of Poland hit the headlines of every newspaper.

People depended on newspapers and radio to keep in touch with events abroad.

The swastika banner became Germany's national flag in September 1935.

The World at War

World War 2 was fought between 1939 and 1945. The main countries involved were Britain and the **Commonwealth**, France, the USA and the USSR (the **Allies**) on one side and Germany, Italy and Japan (the **Axis** powers) on the other. The war began in the autumn of 1939 when Germany, under the command of Adolf Hitler, invaded Poland. As Hitler attacked and occupied more and more countries, almost the whole of Europe fell into the grip of the Axis powers.

In 1941, two important things happened to make the war spread across the world. Firstly, Germany invaded Russia, taking the war into the east. Secondly, Japan attacked an American naval base called Pearl Harbor. This event brought Japan into the war on the side of the Axis powers, and America on the side of the Allies. It was now truly a world war.

In 1943, the Allies invaded Italy, which surrendered and changed sides to fight against the Germans. A year later, the Allies invaded France (which had been occupied by Hitler's army for four years) and advanced towards Germany. Meanwhile, the Russian army started to advance on Germany from the east.

American soldiers left their families to join the war in 1941.

Jews in Germany were imprisoned or killed by the **Nazis**.

In May 1945, Hitler realized he had lost and so committed suicide. Germany surrendered and the war in Europe ended. However, the Japanese were still fighting the Allies in the east, and it was not until early August, when American planes dropped two **atomic bombs** on the Japanese cities of Nagasaki and Hiroshima, that World War 2 was finally over.

In Britain, city children were evacuated to the countryside (see pages 16-19).

Jews like Anne Frank were forced into hiding in the Netherlands (see pages 34-35).

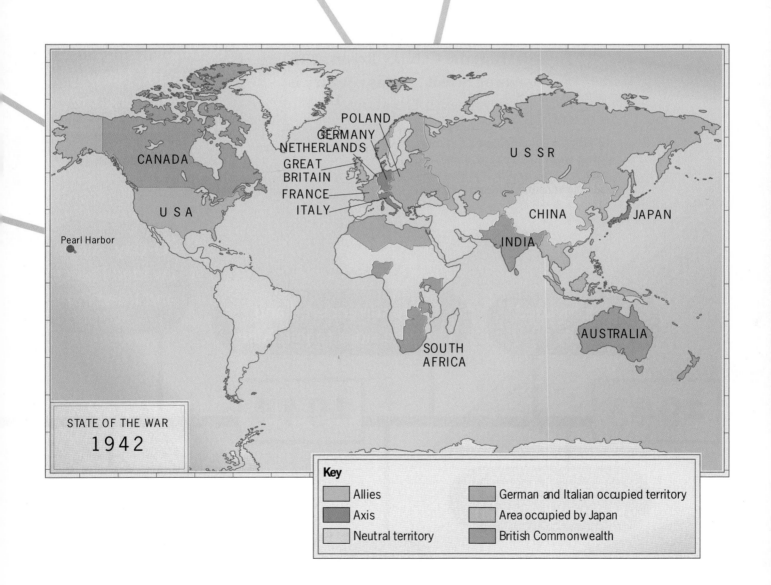

POLAND
GERMANY
NETHERLANDS
GREAT
BRITAIN
FRANCE
ITALY

CANADA

USA

Pearl Harbor

USSR

CHINA

JAPAN

INDIA

SOUTH
AFRICA

AUSTRALIA

STATE OF THE WAR
1942

Key

Allies

Axis

Neutral territory

German and Italian occupied territory

Area occupied by Japan

British Commonwealth

World War 2 timeline

Britain and France declared war on Germany

Rationing started

Hitler invaded Poland

1939

❝ I am speaking to you now from the Cabinet Room at 10, Downing Street . . . this country is at war with Germany. **❞**

The people of Britain learnt that they were at war with Germany when the Prime Minister, Neville Chamberlain, made the announcement on the radio.

1940

Germany conquered Denmark, Norway, Luxembourg, the Netherlands, Belgium and France

D-Day. Allies invaded France and freed Paris

Allies invaded Italy

Italy surrendered and changed sides to join Allies

1943

1944

Germany defeated at Stalingrad (Russia)

Russians advanced on Germany

Allies bombed Germany

Battle of Britain fought and won by the British

War fought at sea

The **Blitz** started

JAPANESE BOMB PEARL HARBOR!

Hickam, Wheeler, Kaneohe Hit

MORE THAN 2,000 DIE IN SNEAK AIR ATTACK

Japan attacked Pearl Harbor

Hitler began systematic killing of Jewish people in Germany

The Blitz continued

1941 ➤

1942

Japan occupied French Indo-China

Germany defeated at El Alamein (Egypt)

War began to go in Allies' favour

British children evacuated from cities to the countryside

Germany fought in North Africa

Hitler committed suicide. Germany surrendered to Allies

War in Europe ended

Second World War ended

1945 ➤

Japan surrendered

Allies dropped **atomic bombs** on Japan

The Blitz

In June 1940, after France had been defeated, Hitler decided to turn his attention to Britain. Between July and October a huge battle, known as the **Battle of Britain**, was fought between the German air force and the British Royal Air Force.

In September 1940, Hitler started bombing London and other big cities, such as Birmingham, Coventry, Liverpool and Bristol, in the hope that Britain would surrender. This began the period known as the **Blitz**. 'Blitz' is a shortened version of the German word Blitzkrieg meaning 'lightning war'. Every day and night bombs rained down on the cities, killing over 40,000 people in total, half of them Londoners.

The Blitz finally ended in May 1941, when the German army turned its attention away from Britain in order to prepare for an invasion of Russia.

Many precautions were taken to try to protect people from the bombs dropped during attacks such as the Blitz.

Aircraft spotters, air raid sirens and shelters

Specially trained people called aircraft spotters searched the skies above the cities for the first glimpse of German bomber planes. When German aircraft were spotted, **air raid** warnings were set off.

Piccadilly Circus station during an air raid.

An aircraft spotter, waiting to sound the alarm.

Tube stations in London were also used as air raid shelters. Often they were dirty and noisy. However, like other air raid shelters, they did not always provide enough protection. One night 111 people were killed at Bank tube station when a bomb exploded on it.

LOOKOUT IN THE BLACKOUT

UNTIL YOUR EYES GET USED TO THE DARKNESS **TAKE IT EASY**

Many accidents happened during **blackouts** – posters warned of the dangers.

Blackout

To try to prevent enemy bombers from seeing their targets at night, the government ordered blackouts. By law, half an hour before sunset, all lights had either to be switched off or turned down, and not switched back on until half an hour before sunrise. People covered the windows of their houses with blinds and curtains, cardboard, black felt or black paint. Air raid wardens walked about every night, checking that no light could be seen from the houses. All the street lamps were switched off and even cars had dimmed headlights.

Evacuation

In order to save the lives of the many children and babies who lived in the cities, the government also introduced **evacuation** as a precaution. Children were sent away from their families to live in the countryside, where they would be safer. See pages 16 and 17 for more details.

Gas masks

The government was frightened that the Germans would use gas to attack people so they gave everyone gas masks to carry. Nearly forty million gas masks were issued in total.

The gas masks were made of rubber and steel and were very heavy and uncomfortable to wear. Adult gas masks were black but children could have red and blue ones. These were nicknamed **Mickey Mouse masks**. Children used to practise putting the masks on in special practice sessions at school. Even babies wore special masks, which covered their whole bodies.

Luckily there weren't any gas attacks on mainland Britain during the war, so the gas masks never had to be used.

Gas masks were uncomfortable to wear.

11

Living with danger

What was it like to live in the **Blitz** and through the **fire-bombings** in Germany?

The Blitz affected everyone, rich and poor, young and old. Buckingham Palace was bombed several times. No one could predict where the next bomb would fall.

Many people were terrified and suffered from terrible loneliness. Some mothers had to send their children away to the country, where it was safe, and many of them had husbands away at war.

CHURCHILL WARNS INVASION IS NEAR

SPORTING FINAL
★★★★★
BID AND ASKED PRICES

The Sun

SPORTING FINAL
Sport Results on Page 40
7th EDITION

VOL. CVIII—NO. 8—DAILY.
NEW YORK, WEDNESDAY, SEPTEMBER 11, 1940.
THREE CENTS.

BUCKINGHAM PALACE BOMBED; HITLER READY TO GO LIMIT

AUSTIN ASSERTS
TALKS ON DRAFT
ARE AT IMPASSE

Says Conference Committee Is Deadlocked on Major Issues.

AGE AND DELAY DEBATED

—KING AND QUEEN VIEW DAMAGE BY BOMB THEY ESCAPED—

KING ESCAPES TIME MISSILE; NAZIS WOULD CRUSH LONDON

Delayed Explosion Watched Two Days Before It Blasts Corner From Building—Germans Threaten 10,000 Planes Daily After Big Raid on Berlin.

> " The **blackouts** were very scary. Especially if you didn't like the dark anyway, like me! You really couldn't see a thing. People fell into ponds and rivers. Cars banged into each other. Some people even put splashes of white paint on their pets so they could be seen in the dark."
>
> *Joe, Plymouth*

> "My brother and I played 'chicken' sometimes. If we heard an **air raid siren**, we'd carry on playing or eating or whatever we were doing. As we heard the bombs getting closer and closer, we'd dive under the table in case it was our house that night!"
>
> *Harry, London*

> "Like lots of kids down my street, we had an **Anderson shelter** in our garden we were supposed to hide in when the air raid sirens went off. We never did though. It was horrible and damp, so we used to sleep under the kitchen table instead."
>
> *Sarah, Coventry*

> "Our house took a direct hit last night. Me, Mum and Will were all in the Anderson shelter. We sang songs and drank tea. Then we went to sleep. When I woke up, they were taking me to the first aid post to bandage my head. Our house hasn't got a roof or any windows now. Mum calls it 'bomb damage' but it looks like bomb destruction to me."
>
> *Sid, London*

British Prime Minister Winston Churchill visited the bomb victims to raise morale.

By Ernie Pyle, US war correspondent

Shortly after the sirens wailed you could hear the Germans grinding overhead. In my room, with its black curtains drawn across the windows, you could feel the shake from the guns. You could hear the boom, crump, crump, crump, of heavy bombs at their work of tearing buildings apart. They were not too far away.

You have all seen big fires, but I doubt if you have ever seen the whole horizon of a city lined with great fires – scores of them, perhaps hundreds.

Bombs and fire in Germany

The bombing wasn't just in Britain. Allied planes dropped bombs on German families, too. In 1945, quite near the end of the war in Europe, the **Allies** bombed Germany very heavily. Dresden was one of the cities that was very badly damaged. The Allies bombed the city so fiercely that they created a **firestorm**. Many thousands of people were killed.

It was the week before my ninth birthday. At 8.25 the siren started wailing. My brothers and sisters and I ran with Mum to our cellar, which we used as an air raid shelter. A few minutes later we heard a series of huge explosions. Our house started to fill with smoke and fire. We had to escape from the cellar – the only safe place we knew had become a death trap.

As we escaped into the street, I remember seeing fire everywhere. People were running around screaming and shouting. Everyone was terrified. Old people, children, mothers, cats and dogs all in fear of dying.

German survivor of Dresden fire-bombing

Dresden, Germany, in May 1945

Bomb shelters

How to make a Morrison shelter

You will need:

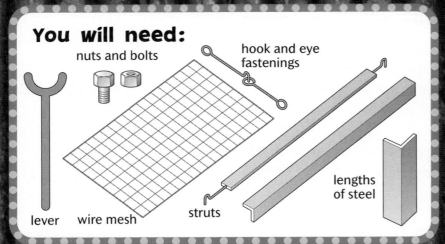

nuts and bolts

hook and eye fastenings

lengths of steel

lever

wire mesh

struts

Morrison shelters were common in many people's houses. These shelters could also be used as a table. Women and children usually had to put them together because their husbands and fathers had gone to war.

Instructions

1

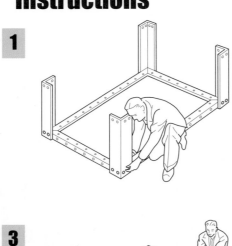

2

3

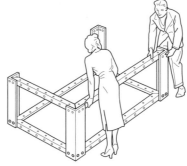

4

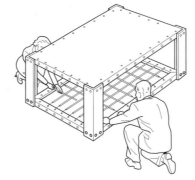

5

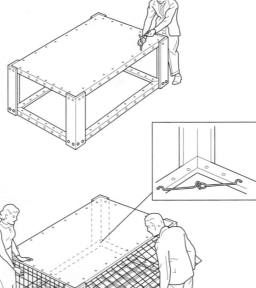

6

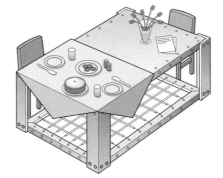

How to make an Anderson shelter

You will need:

spade

spanner

screwdriver

corrugated steel sheets
(supplied)

nuts and bolts (supplied)

curved steel sheets (supplied)

grass

1 foot = 30.48 centimetres

Instructions

1 Choose a place in your garden as close to the house as possible.

2 Dig a hole in the garden 4 feet deep and 10 feet long.

3 Unpack the sheets of corrugated steel and the nuts and bolts.

4 Bolt the six curved steel sheets together to form an arch 6 feet high, 9 feet long and $4\frac{1}{2}$ feet wide. Tighten the bolts with a spanner.

5 Place the straight sheets of steel at either end of the shelter to form a wall and an entrance.

6 Cover the shelter with grass.

Comparing shelters

Morrison
- Space for 2 to 3 people
- Warm and dry
- Used in the home, where many people felt safe
- Difficult to escape from
- Useless if the house was bombed
- Could be used as a table

Anderson
- Space for 4 to 6 people
- Cold, dark, smelly and damp
- Used in the garden
- Easy to escape from
- Provided some shelter from attacks

Anderson shelter

29 April 1942

The siren went off after I'd gone to sleep. I heard my mum calling me to get dressed. I put my dressing gown on and went out to the big shelter in the road. I sat on my mother's lap that night because someone hadn't got a chair, so they borrowed mine. We listened to the planes going overhead. The noise was very near and I was frightened. I heard a whistling sound and suddenly everything was dark and dusty – it was in my mouth, I couldn't breathe very well. We were buried in the shelter. I heard my mum say "Are you all right, Bunny?" and I said "Hush, Mummy. I'm saying my prayers . . . "

Lin Spoor (7 years old), Norwich

vacuation

When the war started in 1939, the government realized that cities were extremely dangerous places for children to live. They began a programme called **evacuation**, which meant that babies and children were sent out of the cities to live in the countryside where they would be safer. The children were called **evacuees**.

The **Blitz** started in 1940, but by that time, many children had returned from the countryside. It was important to protect children from the bombing (some people predicted that there might be as many as four million casualties in the months to come). The government therefore decided that the children had to be evacuated again.

Many families were unhappy about evacuation because it meant they were split up and didn't see each other for many weeks and months at a time. Some mothers were very reluctant to let their children go, even though they knew that they were in great danger where they were.

Persuasive government posters gave simple messages.

The government had to work hard to persuade parents that evacuation was sensible. They published posters to get their message across. In the end, about one-and-a-half million children were evacuated – roughly half the number the government had been aiming for.

The evacuees were sent to the countryside on trains, which were met by people called **billeting officers**. The officers distributed the children among the families who had enough room to take them. They were called **host families**.

Often, the families had no choice as to whether they took in evacuees or not: the children were **billeted** on them and some families resented it. They were shocked to find that some of the city children were dirty and had lice, and that some had no shoes or clothes suitable for the country.

Evacuees are welcomed to their new home in a Surrey village.

Many children were evacuated from London.

Life as an evacuee

Some of the evacuated children were treated like unpaid servants by their **host families**, but the lucky ones were well looked after by kind people.

Evacuees from London enjoying a short camping holiday.

I remember I felt a bit like a parcel being sent off like that, with a label on my wrist with my name and age written on it. When we got to the country I was terrified. Someone took me and my brother and put us in the hands of a rather strict-looking lady. We went in her car down a very long lane. I felt too scared to speak and my brother began to cry. The lady told him to stop it and soon we pulled up at a house. When we got out I remember there was a lovely smell and we were told they were making hay and we could help. I had never seen hay before.

17 The Square
Grassington
Yorkshire

17 December 1941

Dear Daddy,

How are you keeping? I hope you are going to work like a good boy, because I am going to school. It is about ten minutes walk to my school. Leila will find no difficulty in doing those sums you set her.

I've been so optimistic lately that I have made a bet with Anne Parker that the war will be over by the end of September. If it isn't, I have to give her a bar of chocolate (if I can get it), if it is, she has to give me one. Someone told Mrs Farrow he thinks the war will be over by the end of May. I hope he is right, don't you? We cannot get any sweets or chocolate up here. Would like you to send me some in your next letter, that is, if you can get any...

love from John

22 Winchester Avenue
West Pennard
Sussex

10 August 1941

Dear Mummy

They say I'm very lucky to live here but I don't think so. Every day after school they make me go to collect pig food in a big sack and it smells horrible. My room is full of mice. I can hear them scratching all night long. I'm hungry all the time. I'm worried about you and Aunty Lucy and the bombing and I wish you would come and fetch me back.

Ever your loving Babs

Of course it was also difficult for the children who lived in the country. Suddenly they found that there was an extra child or two at the breakfast table. People they had never seen before were now part of their family.

> **❝** I clearly remember seeing them for the first time. They were big girls of about ten or eleven. Their names were Mabel and Pam and they came from Manchester. I was furious! I had to share everything with them, even my bedroom and my toys. **❞**

Early one morning, Ray Chaffey's father kissed him goodbye and gave him his final instructions. No matter what happened he must look after his little sister and not be separated from her. He was only eight years old and did not want to go. He would rather the family stayed together, even died together, than face a future with strangers.

Ray and his sister, both wearing new Burberry coats, joined hundreds of other children on the train that was taking them into the safety of the countryside. After several hours travelling, they arrived at Ilfracombe, Devon. They were taken to a hall and the local people arrived to pick which children would stay with them.

"I was hoping that a nice-looking lady walking through the hall would choose us but she walked right past. Soon there were children getting up from the floor and walking off with complete strangers," Ray wrote later in his diary.

The room steadily emptied while Ray and his sister patiently waited for someone to take them. Eventually, a woman announced that she would take the little blonde girl — she meant Ray's sister.

Eight-year-old Ray knew his duty. He stood up and said to her: "You'll have to take both of us." The woman told him not to be silly. However, Ray insisted and held on to his sister for grim death. Finally, the woman gave up.

Later that afternoon, a 13-year-old girl picked them out and took them home to a two-up two-down cottage occupied by a married couple and their five children. The exhausted **evacuees** shared beds with the other brothers and sisters. They were safe, but far from home and far from happy.

Rationing

Many countries that used to export food to Britain were under German occupation/in danger of being occupied

Imported food from overseas (especially fruit and meat) could not always get through

War at sea

Britain only a small country – cannot produce enough food for all

SI

Soldiers could only help on farms when they were on leave.

War disrupted food and farming industries

Fewer people to process/distribute food

Women (land girls) went to work on farms to grow more food

FOOD SHORTAGES!

Rationing introduced (everyone allowed a certain amount of food; fair shares of what was available)

Government urged people to grow food in gardens and allotments:
Dig for Victory!

Other materials like oil and cotton also affected. Clothes and petrol rationed.

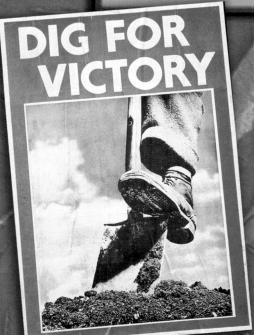
DIG FOR VICTORY

Food

During the war, food, along with many other things such as petrol and clothes, had to be carefully shared out. Each person was given a ration book. The ration books contained coupons, which were cut out and given to the shop owner when an item was bought. This meant that no one could cheat and get more than another person. It also meant that everyone was guaranteed a minimum amount of food a week. Many foods were rationed, including milk, meat, eggs and tea. Children also had to make do with very small quantities of chocolate and sweets.

Here is a typical English **ration allowance**. It is for one person, for one week.

> 1 ounce = 28.35 g
> 1 pint = 562 ml

Hilda was born and brought up in Berlin, in Germany. She says:

" We got three slices of bread a day. Then every week we got 50 grams of meat, 30 grams of noodles and 25 grams of sugar and margarine or butter."

GERMAN POTATO PANCAKES

YOU WILL NEED

- 1 handful potato peel
- 1 handful flour
- salt and pepper

METHOD

1 Take the potato peel and cut into small pieces.

2 Mix it with flour, salt and pepper.

3 Fry in cooking oil, a spoonful at a time, for a few minutes.

English Cheese Pudding

You will need

- half a pint milk
- 2 level tablespoons dried egg mixed with 4 tablespoons water
- 4 ounces grated cheese
- 1 cup stale breadcrumbs
- quarter teaspoon dried mustard
- salt and pepper

Method

1 Add the milk to the egg mixture.

2 Stir in the cheese, breadcrumbs, mustard, salt and pepper.

3 Pour into a greased dish and cook for 30 minutes in a hot oven until brown and set.

Persuasion

So that food was not wasted, the government used posters to persuade people to use their rations sensibly, and to grow their own food. Characters like Potato Pete and Dr Carrot were especially popular.

Dr Carrot and Potato Pete were leading characters in a 'grow your own vegetables' campaign.

Potatoes were easier to produce than bread.

The wartime home

Although in the 1940s cars were less common than today, owners faced petrol **rationing**

Many people used ponies and traps

Steel in short supply – railings/gates cut down and taken away

Rationing
(see also pages 20-21)

Clothes rationing began 1941: clothes recycled; women knitted new jumpers from old wool

- Bicarbonate of soda used instead of deodorant
- Women used burnt cork as mascara

No ladies' stockings available: some women painted gravy browning on their legs and drew a line up the back of each leg to look like stockings

Entertainment

Cinema audiences increased

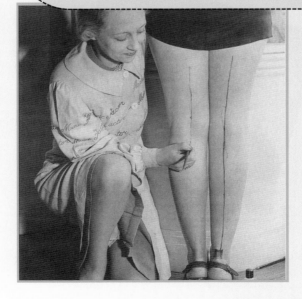

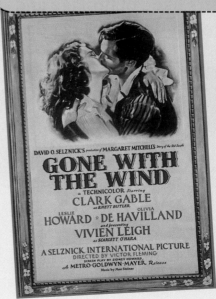

EVERYDAY LIFE IN THE WAR

Women aged 18 to 30 obliged to register for war work

Many women worked in factories

Women at work
Men away in services so women had to take on men's jobs at home

The Women's Land Army set up: June 1939 – women worked on farms

Football continued to be popular

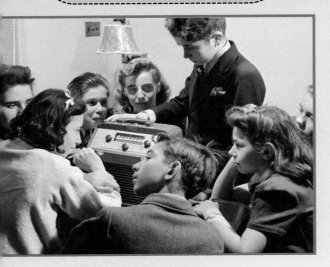

Air raids
(see also pages 10-13)

(see also pages 42-43)

Many sports events cancelled

Wartime newspapers

Along with radio broadcasts, newspapers were very important during the war. They were important for two major reasons. Firstly, newspapers gave information about the war, both at home and abroad. However, the **Ministry of Information** censored this news. It was dangerous for newspapers to say anything about the movement of soldiers, for example, in case the enemy used the information against them.

The second thing newspapers could do was to make people feel better. Newspapers gave a lot of space to stories about victories over the enemy, which helped people to believe that Britain would eventually win the war, and that peace would return.

DAILY MIRROR, Wednesday, Sept 11 1940

Daily Mirror
SEPT 11

Nº11,408 — ONE PENNY

REGISTERED AT THE G.P.O AS A NEWSPAPER

GIVE A HOME - TO RAID VICTIM

Mr Malcolm Macdonald, Minister of Health, broadcast an appeal last night asking house holders in the London Civil Defence area to accommodate people made homeless by air raids.

He asked the public to tell their Town Halls today how many extra people they could home and for how long.

For those who could not offer free hospitality there was provision for payments under the Government billeting scheme.

Mr Macdonald also asked for gifts or loans of furniture and bedding.

More Homeless Yet

He said the bombing had caused fewer casualties and less damage to public services than expected. Numbers of dwellings had been destroyed and there were many homeless people.

In many cases they would be able to return to their homes after a few days but the number without houses would steadily increase.

In the large boroughs were centres where the homeless could get immediate shelter and bedding. There was no barrier to prevent any borough from helping another. The task was one that London must solve as a whole.

Many of the homeless from the more pressed areas were being accommodated in other districts.

CLOUD DODGERS IN 4TH BLITZ

AFTER Goering had four times sent reconnaissance planes dodging through the clouds to London yesterday, the area's fourth successive night raid started at 8.14.

It was London's fifth "alert" signal of the day. None of the previous warnings lasted more than half an hour, and the third lasted only eighteen minutes.

Said an Air Ministry and Ministry of Home Security communique:

"At various times during the afternoon a few enemy aircraft making use of cloud cover, penetrated to the London area. They were apparently on reconnaissance and no bombs are reported to have been dropped in this area."

"One of the enemy bombers was shot down by our fighters."

In the night raid German machines penetrated London's defences and dropped a number of incendiary bombs on north-west and south-west London.

The enemy airmen had no blazes to guide them this time and up to seven o'clock confined their raiding to the outskirts of London from which gun flashes and occasional explosions could be seen.

Then activity increased, and as searchlights swung over the sky three high explosive bombs went off with a shattering roar in one district–and three more in other districts.

Flying Glass Injures One in Five

Though only one case is known of a person being killed by flying glass in air raids on Britain, one in every five of the cases of injury have been caused by this means.

A Ministry of Home Security expert said this in a broadcast last night on the effect of blast from bombs falling among houses.

Curtains and blinds, he said, would do little to stop glass from flying, but there were several good ways of protecting windows. A strong Black-out screen covered with building boards or plywood was one, but that would be in position only at night. By day a fine-mesh wire netting would stop all but a few small pieces of glass.

Use Less Water in Your Bath

Less water must be used for baths, washing up and the garden.

Upmost economy on water is urged on all consumers by the Metropolitan Water Board to enable essential work to be done, and the supply restored to its full quantity.

SPLITTING HEAD?

GENASPRIN KILLS PAIN QUICKLY–TIME IT.

'Genasprin' works quickly because of its absolute purity and complete split-second disintegration. Doctors recommend 'Genasprin' It cannot upset your digestion or your heart.

At every time of strain or pain 'GENASPRIN' sees you through

As the war went on, more people started reading newspapers. It was a way of keeping in touch with events abroad.

Because of the shortage of paper to print newspapers on, many newspapers were reduced to just four pages during the war. Newspaper editors could therefore print only the most important news.

Daily Mirror

MAY 8

Tuesday, May 8, 1945
No. 12,911   ONE PENNY
Registered at G.P.O. as a Newspaper.

VE-DAY!

IT'S OVER IN THE WEST

TODAY is VE-Day—
the day for which the British people have fought and endured five years, eight months and four days of war.

With unconditional surrender accepted by Germany's last remaining leaders, the war in Europe is over except for the actions of fanatical Nazis in isolated pockets, such as Prague.

The Prime Minister will make an official announcement—in accordance with arrangements between Britain, Russia and the U.S.— at 3 o'clock this afternoon. ALL TODAY AND TOMORROW ARE PUBLIC HOLIDAYS IN BRITAIN, IN CELEBRATION OF OUR VICTORY.

We also remember and salute with gratitude and pride the men and women who suffered and died to make triumph possible—and the men still battling in the East against another cruel enemy who is still in the field.

VE-SCENE
TRAFALGAR SQUARE

It was a high old time in Trafalgar-square last night. Everybody wanted to climb something. This party of Wrens and Allied soldiers celebrated by clambering on to the lions. Army policemen present—like Nelson on his column—turned a blind eye.

London had joy night

"Daily Mirror" Reporter

PICCADILLY CIRCUS, VE-EVE.

THIS is IT—and we are all going nuts! There are thousands of us in Piccadilly-circus. The police say more than 10,000—and that's a conservative estimate.

We are dancing the Conga and the jig and "Knees up, Mother Brown," and we are singing and whistling, and blowing paper trumpets.

The idea is to make a noise. We are. Even above the roar of the motors of low-flying bombers "shooting up" the city.

We are dancing around Eros in the black-out, but there is a glow from a bonfire up Shaftesbury-avenue and a news reel cinema has lit its canopy lights for the first time in getting on for six years.

A huge V sign glares down over Leicester Square. And gangs of girls and soldiers of all the Allied nations are waving rattles and shouting and climbing lamp - posts and swarming over cars that have become bogged down in this struggling, swirling mass of celebrating Londoners.

We have been waiting from two o'clock to celebrate. We went home at six when it seemed that the news of VE-Day would never come, but we are back now.

And on a glorious night we are making the most of it. A paper-hatted throng is trying to pull me out of this telephone box now. I hold the door tight, but the din from Piccadilly Circus is drowning my voice.

It is past midnight. We are still singing. A group of men liberated from German prison camps are yelling—"Roll out the Barrel."

"We sang it when we went to France in 1939 and we sang it as we tried to get out in 1940," they told me. "Now we sing it for victory."

Amid terrific cheers a New Zealand sailor climbed on the bonnet of a bus and from there to the roof.

He stood there swaying above the crowds as the American army swarmed up

Continued on Back Page

War winners broadcast today

You will hear the voices of the King, Field-Marshals Montgomery and Alexander, and General Eisenhower when they broadcast over the B.B.C. Home Service tonight.

After the King's speech, at 9 p.m. and separated from it by the news bulletin, comes "Victory Report," a special programme which will contain the recorded voices of Ike and Monty, and other famous personalities of the war.

Additional features of the B.B.C. Home programme, which will end at 2 a.m. tomorrow, include, at 8 p.m., an address by the Archbishop of Canterbury at a Thanksgiving Service for Victory, and at 8.30 a tribute to the King.

Propaganda

Wartime propaganda

To help win the war, the government tried to influence the way people felt and behaved. To do this they set up a **Ministry of Information** to get their messages across. Information aimed at influencing people's thoughts and opinions is known as 'propaganda'.

Giving information

Raising morale

One important reason for using propaganda was to raise morale. The government knew that to win the war it needed to keep people feeling cheerful and positive. This wasn't easy at a time when many women and children were living without their husbands and fathers, not knowing if and when they would return from the war. It was therefore important to persuade people that Britain and her allies would win the war.

It was also important to give factual information that would keep the population safe and healthy, so that people could carry on in spite of the hardships and **rationing**. To achieve this, the Ministry of Information published recipes explaining how to make the most of food rations. The government also had to make sure everyone knew what to do in case of an **air raid** or gas attack.

Changing behaviour

Another sort of propaganda was aimed at persuading people to change their behaviour or act in a certain way. This included advice on how to stay fit and healthy. It also aimed to prevent people from doing anything that helped the enemy.

All these messages had to be presented in a way that made it easy for everyone to understand. The Ministry of Information invented slogans, and put them on posters and pamphlets. The posters were often funny, and brightened up dull wartime buildings. Most people listened to the radio, so broadcasts were used to spread the messages, too. Slogans and pictures were also printed on collectable cards inside packets of cigarettes: adults bought the cigarettes and gave the cards to children.

The government was very worried about spies discovering British secrets, so everyone was asked not to talk to strangers. To help people remember to be secretive, a famous wartime slogan was encouraged: 'Keep Mum!'

Wartime leaders

Great wartime leaders, like Winston Churchill, made powerful speeches and visited the people to persuade them to carry on the fight against the enemy. Churchill (1874–1965) became prime minister of Britain in 1940. He managed to inspire the British public to believe that the war would be won, even at the most difficult times and in spite of the terrible things that were happening.

George VI, the father of Queen Elizabeth II, and his wife, Queen Elizabeth, visited many of Britain's bombed cities during the war, giving encouragement, support and sympathy to those living in the wreckage.

When the war had finally ended, King George VI sent this letter to every schoolgirl and boy in Britain.

King George and Queen Elizabeth visit a bombed city.

8th June, 1946

To-DAY, AS WE CELEBRATE VICTORY, I send this personal message to you and all other boys and girls at school. For you have shared in the hardships and dangers of a total war and you have shared no less in the triumph of the Allied Nations.

I know you will always feel proud to belong to a country which was capable of such supreme effort; proud, too, of parents and elder brothers and sisters who by their courage, endurance and enterprise brought victory. May these qualities be yours as you grow up and join in the common effort to establish among the nations of the world unity and peace.

George R.I.

Even in the bleakest days of the war, Churchill inspired the people of Britain to keep on fighting. He used a V sign for victory, which soon caught on across the nation.

"We shall go on to the end, we shall fight in France, we shall fight on the seas and oceans, we shall fight with growing confidence and growing strength in the air, we shall defend our Island, whatever the cost may be, we shall fight on the beaches, we shall fight on the landing grounds, we shall fight in the fields and in the streets, we shall fight in the hills; we shall never surrender . . ."

Great leaders like Churchill made speeches to persuade people to carry on the fight against the enemy.

"I expect that the **Battle of Britain** is about to begin. Upon this battle depends the survival of Christian civilization ... The whole fury and might of the enemy must very soon be turned on us. Hitler knows that he will have to break us in this Island or lose the war. If we can stand up to him, all Europe may be free and the life of the world may move forward into broad, sunlit uplands. But if we fail, then the whole world, including the United States, including all that we have known and cared for, will sink into the abyss of a new Dark Age ... Let us therefore brace ourselves to our duties, and so bear ourselves that, if the **British Empire** and its **Commonwealth** last for a thousand years, men will still say, 'This was their finest hour'."

The content of Churchill's speeches, together with his deep, gravelly voice, inspired hope and belief that the war would be won.

31

Refugees

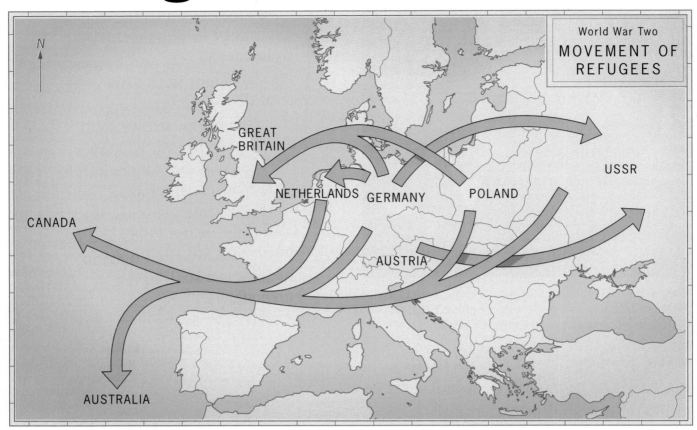

During the war, many people from many countries were forced to leave home and escape to new countries where they would be safer. It was a frightening experience. Many of these **refugees** were tiny babies and little children.

The boat was scary. The only grown-ups were soldiers and nurses. I remember seeing the white cliffs of Dover. It was a beautiful sight.

In 1943 I arrived in Persia on a train from Siberia with thousands of other children. Just children, no parents. No adults except the soldiers. I remember nothing now about Siberia except snow and being cold and a little piglet that was my only friend. When I woke crying in the night I would always be crying, "they are taking the piglet from me ... mama ... mama ... they are taking the piglet ..." and my mother who was not my mother would kiss me and hold me until I fell asleep again.

Kindertransport

At the beginning of the war, 10,000 Jewish children, who were in great danger, were rescued from Germany, Austria and Czechoslovakia. They were taken on trains and boats to start new lives in Britain. It was a plan called *kindertransport*, a German word meaning 'child transport'. Most of the children left without their parents and the journeys were long and tiring. Sadly, many never saw their parents again.

"They pushed me on to the train and I wasn't even allowed to say goodbye to Mum and Dad."

"I was put on a Kindertransport in April 1939. My strongest memory of the trip was the hold of the ship, illuminated by bare bulbs, and Red Cross nurses giving us tea throughout the night."

"Unlike most of the other kids, my brother and I were fluent in English, so we weren't too scared. We were luckier than most."

"All I remember about the train is passing hundreds of platforms and seeing thousands of swastikas."

"I had already discovered that when you are unsure, or afraid, it was best to keep silent. I had said nothing to my parents about what was happening to me at school; the jostling, which was supposedly accidental, followed by the grinning, insincere apology, the foot jerked out suddenly as I passed between the rows of desks, so that I stumbled and fell. And the whispered word, 'Jew, Jew, Jew …' Sometimes the sound followed me all day."

It was not just Jewish people who were affected by the war and forced to flee to other countries. German civilians were also bombed out and forced to leave their homes and cities in search of safer places to live.

Anne Frank

Throughout World War 2, people all over the world were horrified at the way Hitler was treating Jewish people. Many wanted to help Jewish families but it was an extremely dangerous thing to do. Some families risked everything, even their own lives, to protect Jewish families from being imprisoned and murdered by Hitler's **Nazis**. Other families tried to help but were found out and punished or killed. In total, a million and a half Jewish children died during the war.

Many Jewish people escaped from Germany, Austria and Czechoslovakia and went to hide in countries like France, Holland and Belgium. Even when they had managed to escape, life for them was terrible. They were in constant danger of being discovered and arrested, punished or killed. They lived in secret, never going out, relying on the kindness of other people to feed them and to give them a place to live.

The most famous of these Jewish children was a little girl called Anne Frank. Anne was forced to go into hiding in Holland during the **Holocaust**. She and her family, along with four others, spent just over two years in some rooms above her father's office in Amsterdam. This is her story:

1933 Anne, aged 4, left Germany for Amsterdam.

1933-40 Anne went to school in Amsterdam and made new friends.

1940 Hitler invaded Holland. The Frank family were in danger.

August 1944 Nazi policemen arrived at the hiding place after a phone call. Anne and her family were sent to prison.

1942 The Franks went into hiding in the rooms above Otto Frank's office.

October 1944 Anne and her sister, Margot, were sent to Bergen-Belsen, a **concentration camp**.

Anne died of **typhus**.

Anne Frank's diary

We know about Anne Frank's life because she kept a diary. She kept her diary a secret from everyone, even her own family. After her death, the diary was saved by one of the people who helped the Franks. It was first published in 1947 and is now one of the most widely read books in the world. Here are some extracts from it.

The Frank family in 1940. Anne is third from the right

A selection of Anne's diaries and letters

5 July, 1942

Father began to talk about going into hiding. He said it would be very hard for us to live cut off from the rest of the world.

9 October, 1942

Our many Jewish friends and acquaintances are being taken away . . . We assume that most of them are being murdered.

19 November, 1942

Night after night green and grey military vehicles cruise the streets. They knock on every door asking whether any Jews live there . . . no one is spared. The sick, the elderly, children, babies and pregnant women . . . all are marched to their deaths.

3 February, 1944

I've reached the point where I hardly care whether I live or die. The world will keep on turning without me, and I can't do anything to change events anyway. I'll just let matters take their course and concentrate on studying and hope that everything will be all right in the end.

5 April, 1944

When I write, I can shake off all my cares.

11 April, 1944

The time will come when we'll be people again and not just Jews!

Wartime children

Children from Cornwall to Scotland and Wales to
East Anglia were affected in various ways by the war.

Janet in Glasgow

"I was only a baby when the war started
so I don't remember much except one
thing that happened after the war had
ended and I saw my first banana!
I couldn't believe it was edible. I didn't
know what it was."

Sheila in Abergavenny

"The best thing about the war was
meeting Katie. She was an **evacuee**
from London and we got on like a
house on fire."

Trevor in Burford, the Cotswolds

"I remember my mum telling me to
hurry up and finish my breakfast
because there were loads of little
children from London coming and
then she said we were going to get
one. I thought it was brilliant. I didn't
have any brothers or sisters and I
really wanted someone to play with."

David in Manchester

"Me and my mate Billy we saw this bomb once just lying in the gutter. We started rolling it down the street, just for a laugh, really. Then someone shouted really loudly 'Leave that bomb alone, you tartars!' and we ran off really fast."

Billy in Birmingham

"I was fifteen in 1941 and I remember being angry that I wasn't old enough to go off to war and fight. I thought there had to be something I could do. My dad was on firewatching duty every night so I thought the National Fire Service would be a good place for me to start. I loved doing my bit."

Mary in Plymouh

"Terrified's the only way to describe it. I was a mum with two little kids – a girl and a boy – and I had to send them away to some strange family I'd never met in case we got bombed. I was so relieved when they finally came home again. You can't imagine what it's like putting your kids on a train in the middle of a war."

Joyce in York

"We all had to carry **gas masks** around all the time. At school we had special practice in putting them on and then going out to the **air raid** shelter. We thought it was great because it interrupted the lesson and we got to go outside. I remember one boy was scared of his gas mask so they gave him a **Mickey Mouse gas mask**."

Peter in London

"One night we didn't make the shelter in time so I just lay down in the kitchen because a bomb had fallen just down the road. The whole house shook, even the glass in the windows. I thought it was going to shatter. And then it all went very quiet and I started to cry."

Research project

How can you find out more about World War 2 in your area? Clues and sources can be found all over the place. You just need to know where to look! Here are some suggestions for you.

Coventry Cathedral after an air raid in November 1940

- ⟳ Your school may have played a part in the war. Ask around to see if there are any old records or documents. School registers can tell you how many **evacuees** attended the school and how long they stayed there.

- ⟳ Go to the local library and ask to see letters, records and photos of the area during the war. The library will also have local history books you can consult. Compare the photos with the way your town or village looks today.

The ruins of Coventry Cathedral today, with the new cathedral in the background

- ⟳ Look carefully at rows of houses. See if you can spot a newer looking house in a row of older houses. If you can, it may be a 'bomb hole', which indicates that a house was destroyed and a new house built in its place.

- ⟳ Look at war memorials. They will often give you the names of people who fought and died or went missing in the war. See if you recognize any local names. Perhaps you might know a family with the same name.

- ⟳ Visit your local record office and museum.

War memorial

- Ask to see the register in your local parish church.

- Grandparents and parents may have objects such as ration books, photos or letters that you can look at.

Wartime objects may be fragile. Handle them with care.

- See if you can spot any low sheds in gardens. They could be the remains of an **Anderson shelter** or a local **air raid shelter**.

- Your local newspaper will almost certainly have an archive of old editions.

- You may still be able to see concrete pillboxes in fields or along the coast. They were built as defences in World War 2.

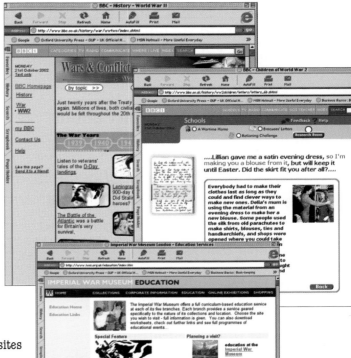

- Do a search on the Internet for wartime memories, photos and records from your town or village.

Internet websites

Questions to ask someone who lived through the war

- What's your strongest memory of the war?
- What was the worst food you had during the war? And the best?
- Did you have a **Mickey Mouse gas mask**?
- Did you have an air raid shelter at home or did you use a public one?
- Were you evacuated? If so, where to?
- Can you describe what it was like to be an evacuee?
- Did any evacuees come to stay with you?
- Did you work in the war? What did you do?

Everyday life

Channel 4 conducted an experiment to see exactly what life was like for people who lived through World War 2. They chose an ordinary family to live in a 1940s house for three months. The family were the Hymers from a small town called Otley, near Leeds. Ben (aged 10) and Thomas (aged 7) told us what they thought of their experience:

What was the best part about being in the 1940s house?

Thomas: The best part of being in the 1940s house was being head gardener. I liked getting dirty and watching things grow.

Ben: I especially liked sitting in the Spitfire at Biggin Hill airshow. It was a once-in-a-lifetime opportunity, as was the whole programme.

Thomas: I liked being in the **Anderson shelter** playing games with my family but I didn't like getting up in the middle of the night. My chicken-wire bed (in the shelter) was very comfy though.

Ben: I liked building the Anderson shelter and all getting together as a family at night in the Anderson. Even though we knew there were no real bombs it was still very scary – not very comfortable beds I might add.

Ben and Thomas in the Anderson shelter. They had to build the shelter exactly as people did during World War 2.

What was the worst part about being in the 1940s house?

Thomas: There was nothing in the 1940s house that I didn't like except Granny's salty soup.

Ben: I didn't like the shortages of sweets and food and I despised the itchy clothes and also I disliked the siren as it symbolized the terror of war – people dying.

How did you wash your clothes?

Ben: I didn't wash them very often but my mum and grandma took the clothes and stoked (boiled) them and then put them through a mangle.

The boys' mother, Kirstie, and grandmother, Lyn, putting clothes through the mangle.

What was the bathroom like?

Thomas: In the bath there was a line round the inside so we didn't waste water.

Kirstie showing how much water they could have in the bath

Ben and Thomas playing cards and their grandfather, Michael, reading a magazine. They had a radio but no television.

Planning meals was difficult because of food **rationing**. The Hymers did not have ready-made meals or a microwave.

What food/dishes did you miss?

Ben: Pasta and stuff like that – sweets and stuff but food wasn't as bad as everyone thinks – similar to today's food but not as tasty – no additives.

What did you do for fun?

Thomas: We played football outside and made stuff – a puppet show.

Ben: We played football a lot and made up games. We had some board games but made up games from nothing. We listened to the radio – I liked **ITMA**.

Keeping the peace

Once the war was over, everybody realized that there was still a huge amount of work to be done. Terrible suffering had been caused, cities ruined and millions of people killed. So the most important thing of all was to prevent another world war from ever happening again. It was decided that countries should form a kind of club where they could work together with the common aim of keeping peace in the world.

United Nations

The idea was that even if countries disagreed with each other (over things like frontiers or trade) then instead of fighting with each other the 'club' would be there as a place where they could discuss the problems. They could also get other countries to help them find a solution.

The club was called the United Nations Organization and it was formed on 24 October 1945. Fifty-one countries joined that year. Since then, more and more countries have joined and so far the United Nations has 189 members.

People from 50 nations met in San Francisco to agree on the Charter of the United Nations on 24 October, 1945.

UN soldiers on patrol

Europe

Six European countries, some of which had been enemies during the war, decided that a good way of preventing war was to share their production of steel and coal. Steel and coal were the two materials most used for making weapons and tanks. So in 1951, France, Italy, Germany, Holland, Belgium and Luxembourg formed the European Coal and Steel Community.

Over the years, this organization grew and changed, and became the European Union. By 2002 it had 15 member countries. For over 50 years, there have been no more wars in western Europe.

The European Union headquarters in Brussels

The flag of the European Union

Key

Original members of the European Union

Members of the European Union in 2002

Glossary

air raid an attack by aircraft dropping bombs

air raid sirens sirens that warned people to take cover because the German air force had been seen approaching the coast of Britain

Allies Britain and the Commonwealth, France, the USA and the USSR

Anderson shelter outdoor air raid shelter made of steel

atomic bomb a very powerful bomb made of uranium and plutonium

Axis countries Germany, Italy and Japan

Battle of Britain a huge battle fought in June 1940 between the British Royal Air Force and the German air force

billet to give an order to people to house children from the cities

billeting officers people who met arriving evacuees at stations and allocated them to families

blackouts the switching out of lights to prevent bombers from seeing their targets

Blitz Hitler's campaign to bomb London and other big cities between 1940 and 1941

British Empire all the countries that were ruled by Britain

Commonwealth a group of countries united by a common interest or history

concentration camps the places Hitler sent Jews to in order to kill them

D-Day 6 June 1944, the day of the Allied invasion of France, leading to the liberation of Paris (25 August) from German occupation

evacuation the act of moving people to a place of safety

evacuees people who are moved to places of safety

fire-bombings the dropping of bombs that were specially designed to cause fires

firestorm a huge blaze of fire caused by heavy bombing

gas masks masks designed to protect people from breathing dangerous gases

Holocaust the mass murder of Jews by the Nazis

host families the families who took in evacuees

imported brought in from another country

ITMA 1940s comedy radio programme 'It's that Man Again'

Mickey Mouse gas mask gas mask painted red and blue for children

Ministry of Information department of the government set up to inform the people

Morrison shelter indoor air raid shelter made of wood

Nazi a member of the National Socialist German Workers' Party, founded in 1919 and rising to power in 1933 under Hitler's leadership

ration allowance the quantity of food allowed for each person under rationing

rationing sharing out food fairly at a time of shortages

refugees people who escape from their home countries and go to live in other countries

typhus a dangerous fever transmitted to humans by lice

Bibliography

Non-fiction

The Blitzed Brits (Horrible Histories), Terry Deary and
Martin Brown
ISBN: 0590558250

The Woeful Second World War (Horrible Histories), Terry
Deary and Martin Brown
ISBN: 0439997135

Wartime Whiffs (Smelly Old History), Mary Dobson
ISBN: 0199105308

What they don't tell you about World War II, Bob Fowke
ISBN: 034068612X

The Diary of a Young Girl, Anne Frank
ISBN: 0140264736

War in Grandma's Day, Faye Gardner
ISBN: 0237520087

The 1940s House Activity Book, John Malam
ISBN: 0752219332

The Oxford Children's Book of Famous People
ISBN: 019910977X

Fiction

Carrie's War, Nina Bawden
ISBN: 0140364560

The Blitz, The Diary of Edie Benson, London 1940-41,
Vince Cross
ISBN: 0439997410

The Other Way Round, Judith Kerr
ISBN: 0006712347

A Small Person Far Away, Judith Kerr
ISBN: 0007137621

When Hitler Stole Pink Rabbit, Judith Kerr
ISBN: 000713763X

Eva by Shirley Isherwood
ISBN: 019 917813 5
Goodnight Mister Tom, Michelle Magorian
ISBN: 0140372334
Fly Away Home, Christine Nostlinger
ISBN: 1842702270

How's Business?, Alison Prince
ISBN: 0340850833

Party Shoes, Noel Streatfield

Websites

www.channel4.com/history/microsites/0-9/1940house/
index.html

www.bbc.co.uk/history/ww2children/

www.iwm.org.uk/lambeth/index.htm

www.timewitnesses.org/

www.winstonchurchill.org/

Index